Wild Joy

Ruminations

Wild Joy

Ruminations

Paul Goldman

River Sanctuary
PUBLISHING
Felton, California

Stone Spirit Lodge Productions & The Fifth
Street Irregulars
www.stonespiritlodge.com

ISBN 978-0-9841140-7-8

Printed in the United States of America
First Printing: May 2010

RIVER SANCTUARY PUBLISHING
P.O. Box 1561
Felton, California 95018
www.riversanctuarypublishing.com
Dedicated to the spiritual awakening of the New Earth

For My Children
(two rays of light searching, yet searching)
Daniel and Sarah

TABLE OF CONTENTS

IV.

V.

PREFACE

From a clear, deep heart-mind I have listened, with both ears! Whether the voice of Jalāl ad-Dīn Muhammad Rūmī himself, the Beloved or some other entity of good and holy intent has spoken, that is for others to decide. I have tried to transcribe the ecstatic words which flowed through both my heart and fingertips to the best of my human ability.

I beseech you to let these treatises on wild joy enter the very marrow of your being and dance the juicy essence of you at a quantum level. There is no need to stress, strain or try to interpret precise meaning. Should you be moved, shifted or somehow elevated from your current position, then that is sufficient.

My hope for you is that a word here or a lilt of phrasing there may speak only to you in a way that you have not heard before, maybe an ancient calling to a love, a reckoning of your own divine inheritance, your divinity itself.

I invite you to slip your shoes off and leave the outside world behind as you enter this silent sacred space. *All* of you is welcome here. You have truly arrived, at home at last.

Welcome beloved one.

In Eternal Gratitude,

Paul Goldman

I.

We do act, and yet everything we do
is God's creative action.
We look back and analyze the events
of our lives, but there is another way
of seeing, a backward-and-forward-at-once
Vision, that is not rationally understandable...

Emptiness
Jalāl ad-Dīn Muhammad Rūmī

MYSTIC WELL

Parched from years spent searching,
precious time spent not knowing
exactly how or when I would fill up my cup.

Surprisingly now — no longer a mirage on a horizon
blinding — the mystic well of my yearning
has at last manifested in this desert.

Thirsty as a new born calf fresh to teat, I long
to taste the mother's milk of mysticism. Quest to know
all that is mine to know.

Linear time is meaningless — yet still the sense abounds
that the eternal grains of hourglass sand fall all too quickly
without revealing that which I seek so urgently.

I seek to know. I ask for patience.

Without pales as within beckons. Silence calls
my name. Once. Twice. Again, a third refrain.

Fathomless mystic well, merge me into your mysteries
as I seek nothing less than to spend infinite reveries
beneath the still surface into the silence.

Move me deeper into the silence,
deeper, even
deeper, until
nothing itself
is only a whisper.

MY GOD IS REAL

There are some things I may not know
There are some places I can't go
But I am sure of this one thing
My God is real for I can feel him in my soul

Krishna Das

Lightning struck me — twice.
My skin was supple, unmarred.
I know my God
is real.

What happened now looked
identical to what happened
yesterday. The difference
is in my knowing,

My God is real. There is
nothing in this illusory
state of living that harms.

Wherever I am, My God is real
and all is well.

A life lived in the Name
cannot be other than blessed. Fear
has left the building for good.

My God is real.

I do feel him in my soul.

4

HAVE YOU HEARD

Monks first prayed here in this darkened cave.
I do still hear their resonant voices reverberating
off the damp walls of this ancient ice chapel.

I sit awhile to soak in the silent moments
aware I am not alone:
the monks come and go often
to this place after they die.

Their chanted words connect like a string of rosary
beads, a bridge from then to now. Choose to listen
to their ancient reveries and be surprised.

For in these dialogues that remain, you will
hear your own ancestral voice joining
those not here in physical form. Rest assured
your breath will stop you
from dying to join
them.

Know that within each one of us dwells this sacred place
where we are blessed to go — into silent
reverie with the monks.

Have you heard?

Have you heard the monks today?

HIMALAYAN MEMORY

A sky painted ambrosia — orange, deep blue
and even a hue of purple nestled amongst the clouds
on the horizon above the Sagarmatha valley. The feet
that tread these ancient paths today had been
here before.

Now, each step was the first, each breath taken
away anew. My eyes — my eyes in disbelief —
as if they could not reign in any more
magnificent vistas.

To leave this place ever again would be forbidden.
Frozen remains to be found centuries later, left to
others to derive meaning from life at the top of the
world.

In my dreams, I have so often climbed each
singular progression to the 29,002 foot summit
of the Head of the Sky,
Mount Everest.

With frostbitten fingertips, I have traced the mystic
threads that connected me here to the Source,
my Creator. In a language at once as familiar
as at first foreign, I prayed the words to Tibetan
prayers I had always chanted.

Womb of my ancient birth, I avow to return
to the land of my Himalayan memory.

Where, my hand will once again grace the very hand
of the Master. The pantheon of all lifetimes lived;
life at the summit of The Head of the Sky
will never be forgotten.

SEED OF BELONGING

Do any of us remember when
that fertile soil was first tilled
in our heart? Fresh turned earth
still damp.

Waiting for what was to come next,
each one of us toiled at labors
important by their appearance — whether
just to be sure the next crust of bread would
appear in the larder or to insure a material
lifestyle we deemed to have improbable substance.

Until there came a time, a place unique
to each individual's purpose — to stop, listen
and take notice.

Something in our heart was suddenly different.
Not as if struck by lightning but a subtle change
rippled quiet beneath the surface.

Words may have been spoken in a church building,
maybe just seeing the divinity reflected back from
another's eyes or if we were very lucky: ancestral words
of a sacred mystic reverberated in the chambers of our heart.

There would be no turning back now. Once felt
this seed of belonging to something greater
than ourselves had been firmly planted within
the silent reverie of our soul.

From this humble beginning a new regeneration
of our very life blossoming into
our truest magnificence.

Finally each of us had arrived at a destination
of our choosing; time to let our hearts open
wide with an endless song of gratitude and
bow to pray for future generations rightfully
to find their own seed of belonging.

WHEN SHIFT HAPPENS

On those great days when sun shines through
scenic greenery robust outside my living room
window, I dine on succulent morsels of exotic
origin convinced — it cannot get any better!

Bam! When I least expect it, right between
eyes surprised.

Incoming events drop from happy bombardiers
adept at flying beneath advanced radar detection.
Without warning, I am left to quiver, wonder
and be on the lookout for the next Nike to hit, hard.

Wait.   Longer.   And still. . .

What? Shift happens. The end anticipated forgot
to show up. I cry where is my omega?

And what pray tell is the alpha doing here in this
murky soup of my existence? Shift Happens —
another ending written as factual fiction.

Here I am in the very middle of my beginning
anew. Waiting, ever waiting for the only
constant —

Shift happens.

CLEAR MARGINS

I had not heard the phrase clear margins
before my good friend used it to describe
the benchmark that was set by the doctor

treating his wife for breast cancer. Seems,
after surgery when getting the pathology
report, what is hoped for is that the cancer

has not invaded any tissue beyond the initial
area where the tumor was incised.

My friend sat with his beloved as the oncologist
explained, yes indeed they had successfully
chartered the waters of this cellular misdirection

and found clear margins. He related breathing
a sigh of relief for now and how this feeling
he has heard me speak of — Wild Joy! —

enveloped his entire being and he just knew
the two of them would be okay, as prayers
had been answered.

I wonder where the intersect of clear margins fall
in each of our lives? If we were to be scanned
by some as yet undiscovered device designed

to reveal how our actions aligned with our purpose,
would clear margins be the resultant pictograph?

If not, then what would it take to bring our being
into a resonant field of clear margins, wherein
we knew clearly who we were and the exact

means at our disposal to manifest the life we seek?

We, who are not at the mercy of a proclamation
of clear margins, appear to have the requisite time
necessary to create an entire new bounty

of borderless bliss. Though, let my friend's saga
serve as a reminder that it greatly behooves
us to move quickly about this business

of setting ourselves right — now, while we have
the freedom and the choice to do so.

KNOWN MOVES AHEAD

Today there is a horserace, not quite won
by a nose, but the known moving ahead
in graceful stretched out strides beyond
that which we call unknown.

I see things seen before, only now they
appear before my changed eyes trained
to differentiate subtle nuances, shades of
character, texture and flavor missed

in the happenstance moments which rushed
to and fro as if each one had some very
important place to be.

I wonder if your sight has shifted as well
to where the familiar shines anew, taking
even your breath away — deeper and deeper,
into uncharted territories?

Glory cannot begin to describe where you
and I are graced to go now;
for nothing blocks the view, no past,

no future, no impediment to felicity's flow
in a resplendent resonant field of energy.

Colors sparkle as if viewed the first time.
Can the sky really be *that* blue?

Spring's iris colored such a vibrant purple?
And the fragrance, oh the fragrance, to savor
nothing more than this scent!

I rush ahead as the known soars past the unknown,
in boundless unabashed glee.

SNOW WALKER

Crystalline white flakes had gathered
    this frigid late winter day. A trail
of pristine white lay on the path.

If anyone was watching, they would have seen
    the old man walking along unperturbed.
Disbelieving eyes tried to make sense of what they saw,
for with each step taken the certain footprint
sunk in soft snow did not appear.

Once, twice, maybe the mystery of no imprint
    could be explained away as mere chance.
But there being not a scant remnant or reminder
    of the sojourner's tracks could not
be explained nor dismissed so easily.

Other possibilities had to be considered. Who
was he and why did the weight of his walk
    go undisturbed?

The man stopped every so often to adjust a gray blue serape
    that barely seemed to hold the wind at bay.
With a meager nod, he would glance back
    from whence he came.

Was it possible he was spirit and not of this earth?

His breath blew cold, every fiber of his being bespoke
of his human substance. A rational explanation
	demanded recompense.

Those observing were not in for satisfactory resolution today.
Supposition was all that they could cling to doubting chests.

Could it be that this snow walker had moved
	beyond his body
into a space of presence, a formless place where he existed
at such a molecular level that his very movement
	happened simultaneously?

Similarly, are you and I able to rise above our corporeal bonds
to feel our place in time move so lightly that we too
	leave no evidence?

In rising above our physical limitations,
will we recover that lost part of ourselves
	that remains clouded out of our view
by the tracks we have up until now
	left in the snow?

THE WATCHER'S TUNE

From on high, the view below
looked quite different.

An array of animals — including the one
that set itself apart and above the rest —
rushed to and fro as if very important
business was being conducted.

A quite uproarious laughter filled
the lofty stillness, as the Watcher was particularly
amused by one adventurous human
who kept turning around, first to see

what was behind him and then around
again to sneak a longing look at that
which was a ways down the road,
the *not happened* part of his life.

This dance of Watcher and watched continued;
how long cannot be ascertained for in the
greater scheme of these things, time was
irrelevant — a lifetime gone in a blink,
another birth and death come and gone
in the next twinkle.

Not unlike the days reported when Eve
chose to exponentially increase her
mortal knowledge of her Creator,

The Watcher began to notice a strange
phenomenon as these humans began
to solve their own riddle, again. Each recognized
their own role in stopping the self-created
fiction of separation.

The simplicity of the how amazed
even the Watcher, as each first

stopped!

Then once one stopped, the next and so on. . .
yes, the appearance of busyness stayed
on the surface, no denying.

Yet, as more and more started to engage
in the sweet tranquility of nothingness,
of savoring their own stillness,
hearts all united beating to the
Watcher's tune —

a new dance of risen consciousness
awakened to the universal beat of djembe drums
singing across all of the continents.

The Watcher's smile again spread
across a lapis sky.

SPEAK DRUM

Under the hazy quarter moon tonight,
her taut skins beat a syncopated rhythm
three four, three four. She is telling stories
from the ancestors, faster, faster, faster,
crescendo. Stop!

A new beat begins in earnest as she speaks
softly what sounds like a song sung
in native tongue.

The notes, the cadence are all easily
painted in resplendent form. There is urgency
to her words, a time for action — an arising
from the comfortable slumber. Spotted Owl
speaks from his tree. She stops mid sentence

to listen, translates bird wisdom into another
melody that somehow speaks volumes
beneath the steady beats, one two, one two,
one two.

Feet begin to move in a dance around the fire,
up and down in time and space until dancer,
drummer and drum herself all speak the same
language.

Smoke rises to greet Father Sky. His outstretched
arm lifts bodies from the circle one at a time
to teach each one how easy it is to rise above
limitation. One two, one two.

Smoke, drum, dancer, three four, three four.
No time, no place, nothing, just the drum skins
speak.

One two, one two, one two, one two.
One two, one two, one two, one two. . .

TRUTH HYMN

All I want is the truth now
Just gimme some truth now
All I want is the truth
Just gimme some truth
All I want is the truth
Just gimme some truth'

John Lennon

Words of truth take flight on wings
of adoration, I am arisen again. These gifts
of syllable, sound and lyric overflow
the empty spaces today.

There is no longer a need to pretend.

A keen knowing suffices as each taste
of wisdom renders false gods impotent,
crumbled to dust as the One is renewed
in glorious surrender.

Chance taken again by small leaps of faith
yields a bountiful harvest as I listen
beneath the spoken
to the revealed.

Refreshed aplenty, the newness so often sung about
in triumphant melody beckons.
I awake to that in front of
my grateful eyes, stride gleefully
amongst the white daisies
dotting the forest meadow.

Hearing the truth afresh, I am complete.

II.

*A sleeper sleeps while his bedclothes drink in
the riverwater. The sleeper dreams of running around
looking for water and pointing in the dream to mirages,
"Water! There! There! It's that There!"
that keeps him asleep. In the future, in the distance,
those are illusions. Taste the here and the now of God.*

Green Ears

Jalāl ad-Dīn Muhammad Rūmī

WALLS OF DOGMA

Think if you will what it must have been like
for the early ones who called themselves Christians,

their quest was for Gnosis, nothing more
— certainly nothing less — to taste
the dew drops of Divinity
that showered them daily,

cleansed by recognition anew
the spirit they sought dwelled within,

the journey deeply wrought
required no special incantations nor rituals,

a present mind, an open heart,
these magic gifts healed the
lame, the blind to see closed doors
opened, the deaf to hear
birdsongs as never sung before,

then, only temporary in nature — in the grand
scheme of time — there came a patriarchal
hierarchy of churchmen who felt threatened

by believers solace, secure in their innate goodness,
men and women who shared a common bond
of faith wherein man and woman flourished
as divine equals, mirrors of the true One,

and then one solemn day dogma was born,
where beings of flesh and blood created
myths to encircle, control and quiet
the transformational fervor of Gnosis,

now the walls of dogma have stood for
over sixteen centuries, fearful followers
turned not to believers but to ones who obeyed
edicts interpreted by ordinary men,

mystic gospels had been hidden away,
destroyed or kept secret, dare the populous
rediscovered the truth:

the nectar of transformation indwelled each
person, man or woman, goodness was the
Divine inheritance and the true path to
a soul's freedom was an introspective journey
to the center of a heart beating with God's
rhythm and glory,

let us pray, every man and woman
on this Holy Day of celebration —

listen closely with me, beneath the surface
to the sound of shifting illusion,
amazed by the sheer grace of the moment
when you and I realize the walls of dogma
have crumbled away.

ASCENT

Rungs on rickety wooden ladders have been climbed,
no bones broken nor pratfalls spilled leaving onlookers
to laugh and mock.

Progress in each lifted knee, raising higher and higher
as if signs given from a Master
paid heed at last.

Risen above errant obstacles placed on purpose, a test
to see if these intentions were holy or only short-lived
like another quick weight loss regimen.

Mountain climbers know well pitfalls of too rapid ascent,
oxygen deprivation addles the mind,
as brain cells atrophy — their journey in a moment lost.

Slow, steady as she goes, a mantra sufficient
to this task. Keep seeking, asking, learning
lessons. Ascend.

Repeat, study, meditate, and listen.

Breathe in the silent moments between
each breath. Ascend.

Repeat; hear the sounds spoken silent as
your name is called — once, twice, three times.

Ascend.

WILD JOY

I have experienced times where I
least expected this feeling to pop up,
surprise! It is me, wild joy
— your dearest and oldest friend —

Jump up and shout ecstatic, feel
indescribable energy course through
veins hungry for this happy abandon.

Without shame, do a happy dance. Dance,
dance, dance until your feet smiling beg
both for mercy and for more. Dance, dance,
dance.

Memories of those moments flood the present:
as an eighteen year old swimming at the farmer's
pond with three young women. Into that water
flowed wild joy!

Sitting not at the feet of the Master, yet having
been awake just enough to hear words spoken
as if just for me by someone at the right time
and the right place.

Something akin to hearing my name spoken in
reverence for the first time letting me hear a bit
about who I really am.

Not the judgments I or others make
but the pure golden essence of me. Wild
joy!

This experience waits holy for each of us. Then all
we are asked to do is be available, to be ready,
to listen when our name is called and that moment
arrives. Then we feel that mighty current of

Wild joy! Absolute abandon. And we dance, dance,
dance.

AND THE HEAVENS

opened anew, and She spoke

the words I had longed to hear,
I love you my precious child,
as I always have. You are the
one I hoped for.

Some of you may call foul;
implore that I am all too human,
no Moses here, no fiery bush
near by.

Please go ahead and beseech the Divine,
I have tried, to no avail.

The refrain has been the same:
I love you my precious child,
as I always have. You are the
one I hoped for.

But wait I stammered, I am not Buddha,
Mary, Jesus, Mohammad, or any other
enlightened being;

I am just another human.

My pleas went unheeded too. She revealed
to me who I was and the reason I had chosen
to return this lifetime;

just to learn love,
nothing more,
nothing less.

in that instant I knew
there was no turning back, no denial
that would suffice,

as humbly as I could, I set out to
practice her command:

to become love in all that I do,
every thought, deed and prayer
steeped in pure Divine love
until —

that day has come when there is
nothing left to question,
as there is only love,

pure love. . .

TO FEEL THIS REAL

Transparent window panes waves, bubbles
and imperfections are all visible even now —
one-hundred fifty years past their prime.

Tribulations of both nature and man have come,
gone; to take a place at history's table set with
the finest artifacts found by archaeologists' hand.

What has remained is an abiding sense of presence
in this time and place; a marker set to remind us
of the ones who traveled these roads before.

Like these snapshots of sand and glass, I too
wonder about the impression I will leave,
for others to imagine whose fingers stroked

the wind where I had dwelled. I speak now
these words I want to have spoken at my last hour:

I was here, each turn of the Earth beneath my feet
solid, firm, real; eyes blessed to witness the turquoise sky
drift across the face of my Beloved,
each breath gratefully taken and always, always
a deep abiding yearning to stay the course —
of feeling this real.

ANTICIPATION

of that which is given, which is unexpected;

Today is a gift, white bow tied atop
 a box silver-wrapped.

I set to carefully unwrap, saving the
scrap paper memory.

Upon first peek inside, I catch my breath
for within is only everything I have
ever wanted.

Heart full of gratitude, this day would be complete.
Still, a knowing there is so much more to come.

No longer a need to ask how I deserved such
precious larder, aware that I am receiving all
that has been softly spoken.

My desire set into motion that which is freely
set upon the gold-rimmed plate of plenty
at this afternoon's table.

Each of us has at our beck and call that which
is to fill our longing hearts with endless delight.

No bridal bouquet or special occasions are
necessary; in the asking is our receiving.
In our giving away of all we possess, we find
ourselves.

In this fateful rediscovery of that which is most
precious, we have uncovered the secret
to our own reward.

Now, nothing else is required. In anticipation
we have arrived — at our own completion.

PULL THE SUGAR STRING

A friend of yore recalled how a certain
woman we both knew mentioned a phrase
"to pull the sugar string."

My diligent search found reference manuals
bereft, ill equipped to define what to my ears
sounded like something I had always known.

How strange to find these words to all absent of meaning?

Maybe it was just the grandmother within
who had spoken these words before
to describe the sweet cups of grace sifted
together with flour, honey, oats and allspice
into a cake of glory risen anew.

All I knew was that to pull the sugar string
spoke volumes of those times when
my sweaty hands clung to the sack paper
bag filled with sweetness just waiting
release — for my own two hands to firmly
embrace the sugar string and pull.

That grasp not unlike the outstretched fingertips
reaching, ever-reaching to touch the hand of
the Archangel Michael. To simmer in the sizzle
of angelic salvation for another moment — before
the inevitable free fall back to Earth.

Remembering in slow motion, that delicious
pull on the sugar string.   35

INTO THE LIGHT OF GOD

The morning sun's rays
splayed through the clouds
as God's spotlight beckoned
my heart to come closer.

This Sunday morning I needed
no special reminder, yet I was drawn
to the sheer power of this
revelatory display. I watched

in ecstatic harmony as
angels danced among the parted
clouds, caught my breath
as the nearest sprite took my hand,

led me, a mortal man, into
the light of a new morning.

My landscape changed forever
in the awe of recognition,
though for a slight moment sadness
sauntered over to sit awhile.

How quickly this feeling retreated as
I saw the importance of not how many
witnessed the beckoning of God's
spotlight;

contented that I had awakened sufficient,
in heightened awareness all senses
grown keen, no longer blinded

to the expanded universe of joy
all around —

once again
took my breath away. . .

BIRTHED

She who birthed the seed
of the Universe

birthed woman who gave birth
to each
one
of us,

without this Divine Feminine
none of this dance
would exist.

On this holy day of celebrating the Divine Mother,
let our exaltations ring loud!

A call goes out for every day
to be hailed as another victory
for our Beloved who birthed us all into being,
simply to demonstrate
love incarnate.

May you and yours always be
aware of from whence you came

She who birthed your mother and
all mothers.

Celebrate! Celebrate! Celebrate!
Each day a newborn awakens
so that we can remember
our Source.

All blessings to you Divine Mother,
in your love and grace, we are each one
birthed anew day by
glorious day.

A TENDER LOOK OF AMAZEMENT

filled her face, in an instant the years
fell away and the rapturous spirit
of her youth entered. She was
ready, vibrating with unbelievable
energy.

With oxygen brought from deep within
lungs expanded, veins pulsed with courage,
limbs limbered up — she was ripe now
for what may come next.

No, there was going to be none of that going
quiet into that good night!

Not if every ounce of sheer determination was
to be depleted in savoring the remainder
of shimmering days to be relived second by
stunning second.

The silken black evening gown retrieved from
cedar closet's refuge hung on her frame different
than that last time. Yet, something — somehow
something had changed.

As she entered the ballroom those engaged in
variations of ballroom dance: waltz, west coast
and even a snap of flamingo, stopped mid-step
to admire this woman unseen here to now.

A new deep breath as partners one after the other,
gentleman all, lined up to take their turns swirling,
twirling her about the wooden dance floor.

No beginning, no ending — for in her mind —
this one special evening went on forever.

TASTE THE NECTAR

Once again I am blessed to taste the succulent
nectar lovingly prepared by hands Divine.

Each sweet inhale, another reminder of grace,
atomic particle purity exquisite as each exhalation
returns golden; igniting a fire light in my heart.

I see each of you in your truth — a beauty which false
judgment cannot vanquish. For the essence of you
is not hidden; a fresh breeze blows across your face
       as She who breathes life into your soul,
       brushes your cheek fair
       with a new kiss.

I dance ecstatic each moment to moment as realizations
float white rose petals soft across the surface of my skin.

A fresh knowing that what my eyes first see as turbulence
across a tiny fragile planet is mere illusion, a magician's
parlor card trick.

Thirstily, I embrace your golden chalice to drink deep
again the nectar, the sweet nectar.

The breath again, the inhalation, exhalation, the taste
of everything possible in each drop of air — tears of joy
merge with hearty laughter as once again I hear
your truth and believe —

simply believe again. . .

III.

. . .Why is it now so easy to surrender,
even for those already surrendered?

There is no answer to any of this.
No one knows the source of joy.

A poet breathes into a reed flute,
and the tip of every hair makes music. . .

from *The Source of Joy*
Jalāl ad-Dīn Muhammad Rūmī

AN OPEN HEART AT REST

Tonight I felt deep joy
even in the presence of faith
taking a few steps back to
comfortably rest.

A quiet peace settled onto
her scarlet pillow — a contented
cat who had found a new bed.

My heart soared inside while
a new gentle storm rose.

No grand disturbance led the charge.
A sense of uncertainty of next action, maybe,
simmered on the back burner.

Plans of grace already set in motion,
place settings for seven, readied
as guests unknown gathered
at their own prescribed time and place.

A knowing of their arrival calmed
the stirring winds as

tonight, I waited for faith to saunter
back in, smile at her old friend, and offer
reassurance reverential:

all in its right place, time and purpose
will come, the certainty of this truth
is by divine design.

A familiar sigh settled into my open heart,
each beat a whispered reminder:
rest, rest, and rest awhile longer. . .

BE

Breathe into that space between
your cells, your comings and goings.

Feel yourself slow down to a near
standstill, a place both dissimilar
and familiar—where a voice you know
so well calls you by a special
name known only to the One.

Waves calm and serene wash over you;
a baptismal pool of your own creation.

In these waters, there is no wrong, no
ill intent, nothing from which you must
repent.

Breathe, again deeper. Into the sacred stillness
you fall fearless assured of open arms to hold
you, rock you gently. Feeling safer, fully safer
than ever before.

Breathe into. Fall into.

Stay awhile longer.

Breathe.

Breathe.

Breathe. Be. . .

HEART OPENING

I opened my heart and found
you comfortably resting inside,
as if you had always been waiting
for the right time when I would
find you.

Had I but known you were here within,
I would have rushed ahead, skipped a few
steps necessary to finally commune
with you.

Surely as nightfall turns to daylight, I have
followed the specific guidance I was given.
Encoded perfectly were the instructions written
in a language that until now would have been
indecipherable.

What is important now that I know where to look,
I cannot ever be lost by the finding of you.

Life itself by each very breath shimmers right now
at a magnitude never seen by these eyes, before.

I drink in the morning dew at each remembrance,
sighting and touch of you there within the tom-tom
chamber wall. And I bow to your grace, your presence
with eternal gratitude —

for I opened my heart and found you
comfortably resting inside.

CHANT LOVE

Love. Love. Love.

Were it that easy, I would
chant love, love, and love
all day long.

Challenges would fade to the
shadows as the light of love
lit a new path. You and I would
know each other in a new way.

All would change: the look in your eyes,
the lilt of your words,
the confidence in your steps,
your smile.

Love. Love. Love.

Were it that easy, flowers would bloom
each new day as a reminder of whom
we are: iris, lily, orchid, daisy, baby's breath —
a rare bouquet, a rich fragrant addition
to this day.

Chant love:
Love. Love. Love.

LIFE IS A MEDITATION

of moments — silken silence
woven together from exquisite
cloth, by unseen hands.

I delight in each of these infinite spaces
as nothing becomes; each molecule
is at rest peaceful.

Images sharpen in the quiet dark,
words leap from the papyrus written
across the ethereal scene.

Understanding envelopes the calm,
the one I was at first entry has changed
upon coming back to breath and this
semblance of time.

A conscious choice to remain longer,
longer here where my soul is enriched,
this place where dreams are reality,
purpose happens naturally.

Life is a meditation of moments — silken
silence woven together. . .

LIGHT BECKONS

In the still calm of twilight,
there lies that space between
light and dark. Here, is where magic
happens.

All senses *are* necessary —
to see beyond mere appearance,
to hear beneath the waves of motion,
to taste the crescendo of excitement,
to touch the vibrant energy and to breathe
in the secret scent, all with a keen knowing.

Magic is afoot here in the in-between as
a reverent light births urgency within,
a call to sacred action. When the light beckons,
you without hesitation answer the call.

Low voices chant rhythmic intimate mantras you know.
Your voice — yes, your voice — joins songs sung a capella.
Behind you, a temple door remains open. Buddha sits
cross-legged at the altar before you.

Not long ago, this would have seemed curious, even
odd. You no longer reject your visions; they have been
humble servants who have brought you often to this
twilight interlude, to this holy place you now call
home.

ECHOES OF THE MASTERS

Each of your souls still stirs mine.
I feel the resonant rhythms
of your words pray within
my heart.

The paradox of measured cadence
juxtaposed with ramblings —
the drunken fruit of so many ecstatic
nights touching the hem of
the Beloved.

I too know times when not only
a fingertip brushes that silken garment —
even stellar moments pristine when Her very face
beams before this believer's eyes.

Rumi, Hafiz, Kabir, Tukaram: each of you
in your way calling out beyond linear time —
though sometimes I confuse your voices with

Van Gogh, forget who I am and reach for a knife.

A gentle touch first to one ear and then the other,
I breathe a sigh of sweet relief.

As I hear your voices mingle, I nestle in the lap of
surrender enfolding me; my heart sails on seas
of bliss.

We are joined across the ages, these mystic dervishes
divine keep ever present hungry wolves at bay — their
barking turned toward laughter, tongues to lapping
our bare feet.

Let the day never come when I no longer hear the echoes
of the masters.

SILENT NOTHING

This silence surrounds me now,
I sit in the still awareness of no thing.

Nothing moves within me, around me.

All is quiet as the light dances in waves.
Nothing calms, stops the rush to there.

I become deeper than I was. Nothing
dwells peaceful. I rest. Assured of
everything arising from this place of
silent purpose.

I greet the day ahead with a slight nod
to the truth that sits smiling before me.
I know, as never before, all of this something
I believe is so certain is, simply nothing —

disguised.

This silence surrounds me now.
I sit in the still awareness of no thing.

Listen, listen, listen. . .

MYSTERIOUS SELF

I am large, I contain multitudes.
          Walt Whitman

Surrounded by glimmers of light deep within
my very DNA, I am more complex than
first imaginings would have me believe.

The sum of all my parts does not easily equate
to mathematical equivalents. I am an
infinite array of artifacts, contrasts in
imagination, desire and well-planned
happenstance.

Purposeful events may have recorded their
merit alongside blips of accidental nuance;
both convinced of their measured destiny.

I know certain things. I know nothing.

I invent stories of my past, tell tales out of school
about a future unknown. All that I see in this
hiccup span of time, I affirm out loud is for real,
forever.

Truth like beauty may indeed lie within the beholder.

I see in your eyes — God,
then who must I see in my own?

Left to my own meanderings then, understanding has
quickened and now that the dam has broken free,
a wellspring of knowledge has begun; not a mighty current
coursing through veins set free,

but at least an awareness of the largess of
what lies beneath this façade.

THE LAST ONE CHANTING

Each breath had been drawn in, released,
drawn in and released as the chant had begun.
Everyone resonated a tone of oneness,
a heartfelt connection as kindred spirits seeking
only to know more of this mystery.

This was as it should be, after all we were
engaged in spiritual practice. No room for
cutthroat competition here.

However, every now and then, even in these
sorts of gatherings — accidents happen.

So, it was when the last syllable of om mane
padme hum was to have dropped into silence,
one lone seeker's voice rose above

the promised silence. In that faux pas
of no pause where only quiet reverence
should have dwelled, this poor soul

will be forever remembered by all encircled
tonight — as the last one chanting. . .

DRY LAND

Words come anemic this morning,
needing a tranquil transfusion of
holy wine. Are you in the wafer
of my desire?

Should I commune with you a while
to bathe in the shower of your blessing?
Or confess naked that I too doubt, that
sometimes the familiar path is not sufficient.

I strive to rise above the need of my longing, swim
farther toward sand than weary limbs allow.
Telescopic vision imagines I see a
distant shoreline.

My faith shivers in the damp water, as belief questions
whether what is seen — refuge of dry land —
is only a mirage?

Listen, do your ears hear?

Is it the instructions to unfold your life?
The answers to sift through illusion to substance?

The call to step into the mystery,
unabashed, assured that when pushed to the edge —
this landing on dry land will be the relief
needed for this day, and for the next.

WHAT DO YOU MEAN?

They all came with questions. He laughed
knowing that his answers were not theirs.
The knowledge of this did nothing to soothe
for what he sought was for each seeker to
reach for that glass of AHA!, to stake
their tentative claim as if their very life
depended upon it.

The joy in witnessing this miraculous burbling
from some inner spring in another was well worth
the anonymous price.

He agreed to appear again on a day unspecified
and advised again to look within not without
was the quicker way — that at next appearance
he might look entirely different.

Questions quickly arose — how will we know you?
who will you be?, and when will you arrive?
Silence.

Some stopped in the midst of their next question.
Still others seemed lost, adrift without oar or rudder, not
knowing that the yachtsman's cap lay at their own feet.

I was there. I saw you.
I just knew.

I will be waiting.

SHE SPRINKLED MY SEEDS

An old cherished friend of many
years this lifetime — my brother
of lives lived past — described
the gift of his spiritual transformation.

He explained how his journey began
back in college as a student of world religions.
Each step along the way
brought new perspectives for his logical
mind to ponder, dissect and separate
the prairie wheat from the chaff.

Seeds were deeply planted within
the fiber of his being, each waited
patiently for the time would come;
the way to fruition would be revealed.

You see, there was one for him
as if by divine design, who was chosen
to bring the means to quicken his
awakening. And he waited.

There were the dry years where he wondered
what master he served, even if a Supreme Being existed
who pulled secret strings, and why he had seen
no signs declaring: step right in — next stop
Enlightenment!

Gifts of coincidence and right timing had appeared
as he opened the door a bit farther with each new
person introduced as the next player on this stage
he called his life,

until one delightful day
twenty years ago, a woman name
Dee came into his life.

I heard his grateful heart skip a beat
as he recounted how her appearance
divine brought him to this place of
awe and splendor.

My dear friend realized that Dee was the chosen
one who came into his life with her golden
watering can — to sprinkle his soul's seeds that had
waited patiently for this right time, this right place
to awaken from slumber.

CUT THE CORD

No greater gift than to love something
so much that letting go feels like a fate
worse than that final relief of faded breath.

Therein lies the illusion — by the act of love
without letting go — the very thing that is
the bringer of joy unbounded brings deep
sorrow.

An old song sung true, the harder I cling
to longing dreams of what should come
to pass, the farther I am away from the
amazement to golden miracles appearing

in my own hand. I cannot then see with
open eyes, as all is clouded by down the road,
when will this or that happen and how will
events unfold.

I have become both the burier of my
own sarcophagus and the midnight
grave robber stealing gems of this night;
the sealer of my own fate.

Enough already! Bring on your sharpest
silver sword. For, I have some cutting work
to be done.

I let go of that which I cherish; gift to the wind
the words spilled as acts of love onto papyrus,
surrender dreams of tomorrow, upon all of these

I gladly bring down this sharp shaft of freedom;
I proclaim right now to see with bright eyes,

a steady heart and the strength to remember
the choice: to live free in the love of each
endeavor and let go —

or to cling to the bonds of unholy longing
and live a perished life, bereft of joy itself.

Enough already! I cut the cord.

Joy reigns supreme;
I awaken again. . .

IV.

*If my words are not saying what you would say
slap my face. Discipline me as a loving mother does
a babbling child caught up in nonsense. . .*

from *A Babbling Child*
Jalāl ad-Dīn Muhammad Rūmī

THESE ARE

not my words; I only borrow them
for this short while. You allow me to
take potter's clay to shape letters and scarlet
flowers into snippets of spirit

to fire in the kiln of my heart.

When I am finished with this hodgepodge
thought, true enough a poem of hoped for
relevance may have been birthed.

A gift unwrapped this eve delivered good
news. Once the ink has dried on the page,
my task is completed.

I have no more to do with what happens next
than Van Gogh does with Starry Night at
tomorrow's auction or any other contented craftsmen
watching from afar.

Whether, I know the merit is found in what I have
written in this lifetime is irrelevant. Nothing
here has to concern me anymore for if I miss
seeing you gain an aha in the next instant,

or in your future lifetime does not matter.

The soul of who I am will as sure as Walt Whitman himself bides awhile to those reading *Leaves of Grass*, be cognizant that a difference was made as I graced words from a higher plane through my own consciousness to this page.

With that I bid this writing not so much a fond farewell — but an adieu for this time at this moment — knowing that a difference strived for is a difference fait accompli.

A LISTENING SKY

The words paint a palette of subtle
syllables across the sky. Each one
content to say what needs to be said.

How much harder for you and me
to dance around our stuck consonants
and vowels to reach our heart

that matters most. Thoughts, emotions,
even yesterday, sticks to our tongue
as we try to untie the knots that have

kept us tangled up for far too long.

Days, nights, come and go into the
eternal years of our lives. We invent
vast means of analysis to sift

through the catalogue of our memory,
forgetting more, remembering less.
Years pass unnoticed — some

at the speed of light itself.

Until, at some spontaneous utterance
of ours under the seductive sky,
we again witness how not only
words but stars collide at twilight.

In this twinkling of moment, our thoughts
untangle, hearts unwind and we begin
to speak our own syllables of longing

and love to a listening sky.

MY ABIGAIL

As sure as if I had been called to duty
by my God and country to forsaken
lands faraway with names like Philadelphia,
France and Britain, you are the one who
has been my steadfast adviser.

When my compass has spun out of control,
up was down, south was north and my spirit
sputtered, a horse with a broken leg awaiting
the certain respite from suffering, there you
have been.

Guiding me to a higher purpose, to a land where
both faith and reason resided peaceably.

You my beloved partner in this life came with
a name befitting the aurora you are — the rays of sun
that shimmer on the clear blue horizon.

For a man such as I to be so blessed is a gift
I thank our Maker for each day I take another
breath. I may not have a Jefferson or a Franklin
in this life — but you, for whom my heart overflows
with gratitude — you are surely

my Abigail.

SAVOR THE MARROW

To experience the electric current of one's own life,
to affirm that this is but a glimmer of what exists —
is to live beyond the bounds of this temporal space.

A presupposition of promise is the parameter
by which this valued life is lived. An
immeasurable quantity of unknown

is both expected and treasured.

Yet, another way of approaching this conundrum
is to chase the dragon by the tail, challenge him
to a death duel, and only then begin

to feel something different pulse through defiant
pores daring to come out alive!

Masquerade as a carefree hobo hopping freight
trains, travel as a foreigner wherever you go,
knife in your pocket at the ready should trouble

arise. Live on the road as your fifties forbearers
did—vagabonds hooked on the adrenaline rush
of a seductive danger whispering through red

lipstick to come hither.

Whether captured by the mystery of moment
or the next death defying thrill
certain to bring one wide awake, the quest

is still the same — to savor the marrow
of life: raw, untamed and unafraid.

The road to life lived electric, felt at marrow's
depth, seems fraught with less peril than
the one lived on the precipice of impending

disaster. Which one will you choose
in order to simply savor the marrow
of your own life? Which one. . .

OBSTACLES OVERTURNED

No court decrees, no if you please
your honor. The barren dirt track
had been swept clean, all hurdles
turned over.

Nothing stood in the way, any longer.

Excuses paled behind this new promise,
seeds planted in fresh turned earth now.
By commandment, duty was clearly seen:
to provide water, nurture spring's growth
in this new season of wonderment and give
simple thanks.

A bountiful harvest promised, faith was a given.
Neighbor upon neighbor brought in brass gallon
buckets — each engraved with the words "yes each
and every thing is possible and so much more".

Nothing left but to believe; the cobwebs of doubt
served no longer, released and donated to homeless
spiders to weave their new home.

Green sprouts of imagination replaced what had gone before in the disbeliever's paradise. By the groves, visitors came to marvel, for significant change like this did not go unnoticed.

Once the obstacles had been overturned, there would be no turning back, a clear path in place for all time. Watering can and shiny garden tools set to the side for now, never to be forgotten.

ALTERED COURSE

An intuitive knows when to shift from a safely charted course
along ancient trails marked by those who have gone before —
to a different path.

Whether this altered course be fraught with new perils,
does not deter this one.

We, however, who are by our own design, faced in the unfamiliar
dark with a new possibility; must choose the nature
of these new risks — versus the rewards we hungrily seek
as if a first meal after days without sustenance.

Our measure is how we muster strength, courage and the sheer will
to go where we must.

Serpents, spiders: whatever else appears before, we are charged
with moving forward fearless.

Unlike the intuitive, certain of a meritorious outcome, we must act
without recompense or remorse. Tasked to place one shaky foot
in front of the other, to grow into this fresh experience.

Our joyful solace is in the striving to finally understand —

we are unbridled in our resourcefulness, purely possessed
of a power which when unleashed will propel us forward
to an altered course of achieving our own destiny
this lifetime.

LIGHT WATCH

We are called upon in this generation
— right now — to be the light bearers, to bring
forth radiance from each other's higher self,
thus bathing the planet aglow —
visible from the farthest outreaches
of our galaxy.

Marching forward in unison through
red rock canyons, our eyes transfixed upward to the
night sky — on the right and left —
perched on high gifted beacons of light
arise at the sight of our promenade of torches.

We are called to move swiftly, even it would
seem to some at a quantum pace hereto unimagined,
leaping light years ahead measured now
in months not years as if the very seasons

had themselves advanced — leaves colors changed
today and trees laid bare the next; summer heat
to autumn's breeze, a new emergent cycle
to mirror humanity's sudden shift.

Rapid change will shake the foundations of those
who had relied on literal religious interpretation
to girder their belief systems. Their eyes will see only truth
yet faith, their fair-weather friend, will struggle to convince
the faithful that to turn away is *sin*, which they must resist.

Yet, at the sheer intensity of light reignited by so many,
the known will benignly fall away impotent; as we each answer
the call to see the Beloved's smile in each other's eyes,
beyond to souls of similar purpose, planetary evolution
will happen in one glorious instant.

A new people cooperatively will inhabit near and far reaches
of our strengthened planet as each of us is forever changed.

The future finally will be a new friend
to be greeted grateful, with bountiful joy overflowing
in each celebratory moment
of lives well lived.

TAKEN AWAY

What at first appears to be a subtraction —
a negation of numbers that had added
meaning by their very existence —

on closer examination reveals a deeper
purpose. Another opening to a different
interpretation wherein two plus two equates
to something entirely unique.

I would have been okay with all of this,
even upon such short notice. Really.

If only the instructor had not changed the
text, directions and grading scale just when
I had thought I was at an apex of understanding.

I am reminded that to stagnate is a far easier
assignment than to grow. Yet all of this
stretching my mind to wrap around altered
arenas of thought has begun to make my
head spin.

To be taken away from a thing that I did not
want is amazement. Ask and I receive!
Only what if I wanted to be the one to pull
the trigger, say caput!, speak the words at the
time of my choosing: "I am done with that"?

I sit with the results, the detritus of that taken
away. And today, with a modicum of fresh
understanding, I bow to the heavens in
deep gratitude for that which was
taken away — expectant at that which will take its place.

CLIFF-HANGER

This episodic adventure has not
concluded. Several possible endings
have been considered but — and this
is important — I am not the final
arbitrer.

I know, I know as the cries of free will shout
out from the balcony. It is as if we all have
our forefather's inalienable rights to contend
with. Manifest destiny and all that, set our
sights on freedom, chart the righteous course
and all will prevail.

You and I know from hard wrought experience,
the determined difference between that set out
to accomplish and the final irrevocably altered
finished product — even of our own accidental design.

Read what you will into the chapters unwritten,
assuredly there are certain to be many a red herring
dropped between the inconsistent pages birthed
at this moment.

At the instant you think you have an astute
conclusion to all of this, the sails set strong
for a northern wind to blow, reverse course
as the gentle breeze of the east rolls in.

Better to keep a steady eye locked on that just
ahead, than to take concern with a history
writing itself; a conclusion
of uncertainty, a true cliff-hanger

to keep the pages of life guessing.

BEARER

I clearly remember when your gift
arrived on my porch just after midnight.
Bright white scissor-curled ribbons gaily
adorned the package wrapped golden.

I sat beneath the winter moon for a long while
patient, in no hurry to untie or unwrap.

Though I did — like a young boy waiting
by the boughs of the fresh-cut pine —
give in to a few gentle shakes to see
if I could discern what lay inside.

That night rested into day as your gift remained
unwrapped; days ensued into months, years followed
as the tide ebbed and flowed in lunar rhythm.

This passage of time was all too easy.

Is it your smile that returns to my lips now?
You remain in memory — as clear after
all these years — as that package still sitting
beneath the oaken mantel,

unopened,
waiting for you.

CAST INTO EDEN

You know the dream of appearing suddenly
in front of your high school literature class
stark naked with all of your classmates,
friends and others, awaiting your stupendous
remarks.

This was something related, though in reverse,
and with a feeling of extraordinary joy.

Fully clothed, on a magnificent sunny day I was
without a clue or warning, cast into Eden
alongside Eve and Adam--who were, of course,
completely au naturel.

I felt like Thomas Hart Benton peering around
the old tree at Persephone. Should I choose to
avert my gaze?

For what seemed like an eternity I watched as
the progenitors of you and me danced, frolicked,
loved and lived fully in the moment.

The oft talked of shame from the tasting of the forbidden fruit
was nowhere evident. Hummingbirds fluttered to and fro.
Butterflies performed aerial pirouettes and cartwheels.

All was divine, in perfect order and accordance.

The desire to remain here cast into Eden was
blissful, yet I knew at the instant of this realization
even as I could not remain here indefinitely

if Eden was what I hungered for, then it lay
here within me. . .waiting.

V.

Listen to presences inside poems,
let them take you where they will.

Follow those private hints
and never leave the premises. . .

from *The Tent*
Jalāl ad-Dīn Muhammad Rūmī

HOW WE DRESS GOD

If I were God, I might have run the other
way a long time ago. I had to laugh when
my dear brother of past lives mentioned
in his eloquent discourse on world religions,
how throughout the ages,

those who called themselves His or Her
children would clothe their Divine Maker
in all manner of garb; from priestly robes
to any manner of fancy they envisioned.

There were many masks applied to this God
as well from feminine mystique to masculine
elder with a beard as long as His staff.

How does our twenty-first century God measure
now, tailor-made clothing? Maybe an Italian
suit fit for an oil sheik or a sleek black Versace
evening gown suitable for a red carpet stroll.

Or as the Enlightened one, being of light, bearer
of all that is love? The one who teaches our soul
to vision Truth needs no mask imposed or
clothing to embellish.

For this One who is above all else needs no earthly
possessions to be love, an enduring love
unadorned, a love sustained
singularly for all time —
a beautiful love unmasked. . .

SLEEPING SAINTS AWAKENED

The earth rumbled this morning — early,
ripping asunder the thin curtain that
separated there from here.

All the sleeping saints slid the stone
away and arose from their deep slumber.

A few yawned, most were wide-eyed,
ready to lighten the load of those who
had remained on this side fettered
by feet of clay.

Much work remained as the harmonic
milieu had so drastically changed since
last saints had supped that infamous meal.

The deep work of bucketing away the years
of religious confusion had begun. False beliefs
were to be deconstructed, ironic idols destroyed
and sight had to be restored.

A beginning would be the impetus to an exponential
shift — in every way equal to this morning's tremor.

New thoughts would enter the arena, each as enthralling
as those that would follow. A thorough excavation
of soul memory would wipe out the remnants of disbelief
in what was known and an embracing of what was
unknown would be paramount.

The old hierarchical order ruled on the vertical axis
was finished. A new holocracy giving credence to
the interconnectedness of atom-cell-organism-
biosphere-universe-beyond and on to God has arisen
on this day, when the saints have awakened.

INNER EYES OPENED

No longer can we trust only the senses
we see, hear, taste, smell and touch.
The vital information they provide
is important, yet for the next wave
of enlightenment — here now just as certain
as the setting sun, next moon rise
and star-filled sky — we must change.

We have the tools: silence, intention, blessing
and precious time. There is no other option.

Turning inward we find the mystery we have been
seeking out there most often to no avail. A grand
paradox waits as our outer eyes gently close.

With practiced patience we begin to find our inner
eyes belong only to us, the key to their opening lies
deep within our being. We might even find lenses
function quite differently here, in eyes that not
only see but smile.

In time and no time, eyes once closed see things
never seen before. We find ourselves wanting
to return to this place of vision, to find a path
filled with white light where we can rest a while
longer.

We become content to learn the ancient art
of mapmaking, to survey a landscape now
as familiar as that we once thought was known
through outer sensation.

Time within beckons more frequently as this
place of peace once unknown, entices us
to stay, to see more than we ever thought was
possible — now through our inner eyes opened.

ARE YOU THE ONE I IMAGINED?

Twilight lit the room as I
wandered in, you sat on the
bed, nary a worry — ageless
after all this time —

you looked not much different
than when you were alive,

maybe the smile gave it away,
I had never seen you so at peace,
expectations lain down,
your crocheted knapsack of troubles
now filled with homemade cookies,

I liked seeing you like this,

I felt hopeful that all of this
could come to a good end,
the day out day in plod of one foot
in front of the other,

yet led to deeds done well
was a pleasant reverie to these ears.
a song of hope poured notes
of contentment from stem
to stern as I righted my rudder

onto a new course inspired
by the vision of you.

BETWEEN THE MADNESS

The voice of the Creator calls your name —
within your own surprised ear — her voice
softly whispers songs of yearning,
you know you have come home,
again.

Between the madness all else stills,
hopes and dreams cherished on the dusty
back shelf of your own desire, spring forth now
as if they were never vanquished.

The all of you feels at a depth you have never
felt before, the very essence of who you are.

You know what is expected of you, and you
demonstrate by letting flow an enriched array of love
unbridled. Loved ones, strangers and foes, step
aside as you walk in grace and confidence renewed.

The farthest-fetched miracles once unfathomed,
glisten on a holy horizon where anything
you wish to transform is all yours, simply
for the grateful asking.

When the Creator calls your name, whispering
songs of yearning — life becomes a gift of gratitude
to be unleashed in wild abandon.

SACRED SELFISHNESS

Consider how taking on a new task
is akin to a healthy food pyramid —
a Zen patterned plate divided into quadrants
of what feeds, nourishes and strengthens me.

When asked to tackle another challenge,
the palate of what I wish to paint
into my life is awash with piquant
possibility. Choices abound.

All I need do is peruse the portions already
bountifully set before me, determine what
must stay, that which is free to go and finally
see if there is any room left for my nod
of accordance.

Only when I can align this truth of time,
will I be in balance. Fair weight without
resistance or remorse given, then I am able
to piece together the patchwork quilt —
of that which is mine alone to do.

Some still cling to a shaky life raft of belief:
that to consider self before service to others
selfishness in the extreme.

Yet, when the evidence is weighed,
a singularity of purpose marked as Exhibit A
reveals how attention to details which might
have been lost in the quicksand of overcompensation
are the inherited value in acts
of sacred selfishness.

NOBLESSE OBLIGE

In our discovery of ourselves we have no lesser
obligation than to serve, shower our innate
light upon a world that has until now shed
a significant amount of inherent light.

Large portions of this planet's populous
still mired in belief systems that shout out
a petulant warning to be cautious,

as if the giant shoeprint on the horizon
dictates it is falling on them.

They have — if only temporarily — forgotten
their birthright, to sing, dance and bay
at the full moon.

Let each one of us then set about to be
the ones to light the fires, burn bright
the illusion of darkness. The dance will
begin again as the bombs stop! Hands poised
to pull the trigger will stop!

Arms outstretched as one people locked
in the embrace of commonality.
Dreams of separation fade as each one sees
the mirror of the other.

Noblesse oblige reborn for a new time.
A holy rite of passage, new bearers of light
united in single purpose:

reveal a new human, Homo Luminous
to a universe awaiting our arrival,
at this moment, right now

NOT QUITE DEAD YET

Awaken! Arise from slumber! There
is work to be done. Yes, your eyes
grown heavy from the early years
of neglect beg per chance to rest
just a while longer.

Awaken! Arise! This is the time of your life
you have been waiting for. Yes, look around
to the almighty all of this. See what it is
you have slept through. The dew on your
eager face is from your own tears of joy,
as realization for the first time of who you are
deeply settles comfortably within.

Awaken! Arise! You have finally arrived. See
every flower, every tree, every being smile
at your revealed presence, your moment of glory
is now.

The temptation to slip back to slumber is there,
though you find now how easy it is to ignore
the errant call to return to whence you came.

Awaken! Arise! No turning back, you sense even
your very atoms sparking you to move ever forward
to rediscover the miraculous details of your life —
which until now had sailed past eyes unseeing.

Let the risen prayer of gratitude sing from your heart newly opened to your own precious essence. Ears resound with joy to hear your own blissful vow:
"I will remain awake, my eyes open to the indescribable joy present in each fully alive moment."

A WHISPER IN THE TREES

Today she went for her first
morning walk, the one
after the last
cold breath of winter —

the bird songs were cheerier
today as the new green shoots
of crocus swayed.

Always more than a bit curious,
I watched with certainty
from my secret perch,
high above the path
still strewn with fallen leaves.

The wait was not too long
for soon enough

the woman stopped, turned
her head just a bit
and listened.

Between you and me,
I never was exactly sure
the nature of words
whispered between oak and ash.

The known was the transformation
as she turned to retrace her steps;
head up, a bounce in her step,
a vivid sense of recommitment,

whatever the message she received, I
was always left with a poignant
longing —

to hear what she heard. . .

PERCHANCE TO CHANT

Poetry has flowed these months
as sure as sweet nectar produced
to keep all the bees buzzing about
their respective hives.

Ecstatic, now I will in just a few weeks
attend Kirtan with you, engage fully
in chanting the inspiration that has been
the backdrop for these words to flow
onto page after page.

Grace has surely led me here to this path
of poetic expression of the Divine.

What lies next is the wonder, the essence
of the passion fruit that awaits to be plucked
ripe for the next stanza, and the next.

I am here. I am ready. I am grateful.

The sheer delight that leaps from my heart
as each phrase turns anew the fount of joy
in full glory; I want these times to last
forever.

Thirty-three years forward when I tap dance
my way into a tenth decade, I intend to still be
centering, chanting and letting these gems crystallize
into gifts — so that others may receive in full
measure that which has been so freely given
to me,

a mere humble servant, grateful to breathe
each breath, again and again.

LOST HIMSELF IN LOVE

Sri Neem Karoli Baba was asked how to
meditate and he replied to the seeker to
meditate like Jesus. . .Master Baba closed
his eyes and became more still than I had ever seen
him. . .until a single tear rolled down his
cheek... he lost himself in love.

Krishna Das

I desire with every nuanced fiber of my being
to be recognized from near or far as a man
who has lost himself in love; to know at depth
my true essence.

Then my smile would reveal the truth of you,
the very love of you, your stellar glorious
magnificence manifested in human form.

Each day, a fresh bite of life revealed — as pure
as a peach-faced mango tasted that first time.
That is how the mere sight of you would feel:
juicy, startling and delicious!

As if I had never tasted of anything so divine
in this brief lifetime.

I vow to make my singular goal to become
that man — the one who has lost himself so deeply
in love that there is nothing else.

Each moment is love, each breath is love,
every devotional chant is love. Hare. Hare.

I give away all I am to you.

I receive pure love.

I give away all my love to you.

I — at last — become the man
who has lost himself in love.

KISSES OF THE BELOVED

My sweetest gift to you tonight
is a bouquet of kisses from the
very Beloved.

My fervent prayer is for these sacred
offerings to shake and shift the
molecular structure of your heart,

wherein the new love you feel
brings tears of joy, peals of laughter
to you, yours and all of your relations.

May the sweet kisses of the Beloved
envelope you and yours for the ages,
never knowing drought, disease or famine;

May you only taste the sweet glory of the Beloved
on your face as you awaken each new morning,
as you go to slumber each evening.

May the transformative power of these sweet
kisses of the Beloved bring the realization of you
so that you may taste the delicious fruit
of your true essence.

Know each kiss of the Beloved you gratefully
receive is magnified as a Holy kiss
to mirror your own divinity
revealed!

May you now go and share the gifts you
received in these bouquets of sweet kisses
of the Beloved.

To everyone you meet
offer these and nothing else.

Go in peace. . .go to share these kisses. . .

AUTHOR BIOGRAPHY

Paul Goldman is a Spoken Word Recording Artist. His CD *Wild Joy Released: The Ecstatic Poetry of Paul Goldman* debuted in March, 2010 to rave reviews:

> "...a tsunami of the soul is sweeping over humankind, and Paul Goldman, with his Sufistic voice is there, fully in the vanguard, helping to define and shape its Divine message of love, healing and joy,"
> — Mark Scheel, author of the award-winning collection *A Backward View* (excerpted from *Evolving "A Guide for Conscious Living"* April 2010 Volume III Issue 2).

At *www.stonespiritlodge.com*, you will find more poetry along with information about the mission of Stone Spirit Lodge.

Future volumes of Ecstatic Poetry, including: *In Divine Repose*, await publication and the next Ecstatic Poetry CD, *Rhythms of My Children* is to be released by early 2011. To delve deeper into Wild Joy! become a fan on Facebook at Wild Joy: The Ecstatic Poetry of Paul Goldman.

www.ingramcontent.com/pod-product-compliance
Lightning Source LLC
Chambersburg PA
CBHW051838040426
42447CB00006B/584